LIVERPOOL LEGENDS ALPHABET

Words by Robin Feiner

A is for **A**lbert Stubbins. This strong and consistent forward helped Liverpool win the '47 league championship – their first in 24 years. He was also immortalized as the only footballer to feature on the cover of 'Sgt. Pepper's.'

B is for John **B**arnes.
After a stellar decade with the Reds, many consider this fast, skillful winger and English Football Hall of Famer to be amongst Liverpool's greatest legends. The number 10 shirt will forever belong to Barnes.

C is for Ray **C**lemence. He set an amazing record by conceding only 16 goals in one season, and won three European Cups. This legend is, without doubt, the greatest goalkeeper to ever play for the Reds.

D is for Kenny Dalglish.
Over his illustrious career,
this ferocious striker earned
the title 'King Kenny.' He then
continued to reign as one of
Liverpool's best managers.
Dalglish is truly a Liverpool
legend amongst legends.

E is for **E**lisha Scott.
One of the greatest goal-keepers ever to guard the Anfield net, Scott will live on as a favourite in the hearts of Reds loyalists after 18 seasons and over 450 shot-stopping appearances.

F is for Robbie Fowler. Nicknamed 'God,' this striker was ruthless in front of the goal. He netted 183 times in 369 appearances, and once scored a lightning fast hat trick in 4 mins and 33 secs. Legendary stuff.

Gg

G is for Steven Gerrard. Many, including Pelé, have declared Gerrard amongst the greatest of his generation. This master captained Liverpool to many historic wins, including the Champions League final in 2005.

H is for Alan **H**ansen. Rated by many as the club's finest-ever center-half, the cool, calm Scot helped bring home eight league titles, three European Cups and even captained the Reds to their first-ever double.

I is for **I**an Callaghan.
Ian wore the Liver Bird on his chest a record 857 times during 18 years at the club and, along the way, won almost every possible accolade. He is a true legend and the ultimate role model.

J is for Jamie Carragher. This legendary defender played an epic 17 seasons and 737 games with the Reds. He was an integral part of the 2001 treble-winning side and helped to secure the 2005 Champion League.

K is for **K**evin Keegan.
This Yorkshire-born striker
was THE football superstar
of the seventies. With two
UEFA cups, three league titles,
an FA Cup and a tally of 100
goals, that status was clearly
well-deserved.

L is for Billy Liddell.
After scoring 228 goals over his 534 appearances, the club practically became 'Liddellpool.' In 2006 fans voted Billy in sixth place of the '100 Players Who Shook the Kop.'

M is for **M**ohamed Salah. After 'Mo' received the 2017-18 Golden Boot for netting a record 32 times in his debut season, former captain Steven Gerrard said, "We are witnessing the start of greatness."

N is for Phil Neal.
For his achievements with the Reds, 'Zico' is one of the most successful Englishmen ever to play the game. This full-back is renowned for scoring legendary goals when they mattered most.

Oo

O is for Michael Owen. This lethal striker and Ballon d'Or recipient is considered one of the greatest Liverpool players. Owen famously scored both of Liverpool's goals in the 2001 FA Cup Final to secure the title against Arsenal.

P is for Phil Thompson. This brilliant defender, who changed Liverpool's style of play, was the first Reds skipper to lift the League Cup. Yet even this was overshadowed when he held the European Cup aloft.

Q is for Matt McQueen. This versatile legend played in Liverpool's first-ever Football League match. He eventually took over as manager, seeing the club safely through to their second successive championship.

R is for Ian **R**ush.
No one has shaken the Kop like Rush. He is the club's all-time leading scorer (346) and holds the record for the most number of goals scored in a single season (47).

S is for Graeme **S**ouness. After seven seasons at Liverpool, where he won five League Championships, three European Cups and four League Cups, the 'Emperor of Anfield' is a must in any all-time Reds XI.

T is for Tommy Smith. The 'Anfield Iron' served 16 glorious years for the Reds and was heralded for his hard-man defensive style. Scorer of the go-ahead goal in Liverpool's first European Cup final victory, he's a legend with true grit.

U is for Emlyn Hughes. 'Crazy Horse' captained Liverpool to two European Cups and an FA Cup victory, while earning himself the Football Writer's Player of the Year title in '77. What a legend.

V is for **V**ladimír Šmicer. 'Vladi' entered Liverpool mythology by scoring a stunning long-range goal and the match-winning penalty to clinch the 2005 Champions League trophy. The perfect way to end his career with the Reds.

W is for **W**illiam (Bill) Shankly. Rebuilding the team with a winning philosophy and creating the 'Boot Room' helped re-establish Liverpool as a major force. Shankly is without doubt Liverpool's most legendary manager.

X is for **X**abi Alonso.
A true Kop favorite and one of the best passers in the game. He earned his legendary status for some dazzling goals from his own half and for scoring one of the most important goals in LFC history.

Y is for Ron Yeats.
A footballing giant in size and stature, 'Rowdy' was the first Liverpool player to don the new all-red kit, and the first Liverpool captain to lift the FA Cup. Ron Yeats was a colossal legend.

Z is for Luis Suarez.
This dazzling goal scorer regularly 'shook the Kop' to its foundations. For his contribution to the Reds, he won a host of honors, including PFA Players' Player of the Year and the Golden Boot.

The ever-expanding legendary library

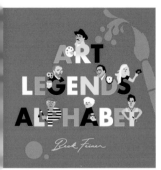

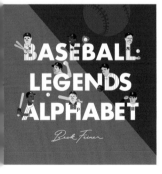

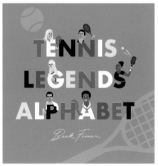

EXPLORE THESE LEGENDARY ALPHABETS & MORE AT WWW.ALPHABETLEGENDS.COM

LIVERPOOL LEGENDS ALPHABET - 2ND EDITION
www.alphabetlegends.com

Published by Alphabet Legends Pty Ltd in 2019
Created by Beck Feiner
Copyright © Alphabet Legends Pty Ltd 2019

UNICEF AUSTRALIA
A portion of the Net Proceeds from the sale of this book
are donated to UNICEF.

978-0-6482616-2-9